MW00341455

I Don't Want Your Job
Is Co-Managed IT services the Right fit for You?

I Don't Want Your Job
Is Co-Managed IT services the Right fit for You?

Bob Coppedge

Copyright © 2020
Published by: Simplex-IT Press

4301 Darrow Rd, Suite 1300
Stow, OH 44224

No part of this book may be reproduced or transmitted
in any form by any means, electronic, mechanical,
photocopying, recording, or otherwise, without the prior
written permission of the author.

The information provided in this book is designed to
provide helpful information about the subjects discussed.
The author and publisher disclaim any and all liability
associated with the recommendations and guidelines set
forth in this book. There are no guarantees implied or
expressed from the information or principles contained
in this book. Individual results will vary.

Printed in the United States of America
ISBN: 978-1-7330048-1-7

Contents

Dedication

It took me roughly 60 years to write my first book, "A CEO's Survival Guide to Information Technology". It became an immediate Amazon Best Seller[1] upon release. Ok, to be honest, it took me a bit over a year.

My second book "The MSP's Survival Guide to Co-Managed IT services" took about 5 months to write and a couple of months to finish it up and get it out. It is also an Amazon Best Seller.[2]

This book (my 3rd) only took about 3 months. Honestly, I should have written it before my second book. Thanks to Robin Robins (Technology Marketing Toolkit CEO and MSP Marketing force to be reckoned with). In a 5-minute conversation, she made me realize that *this* book was necessary. I'd add that she did this without making me feel stupid, but I don't like to lie in print. Thankfully, there was a lot of material in the second book I could repurpose, which made a lot of sense. The second book reaches out to MSP (Managed Service Providers), describes Co-Managed IT services and how to offer and deliver it to their clients. This book simply changes the perspective. This time we're talking to you, the Internal IT person. The message is the same, regardless of the direction.

I've spoken about CoMITs to a couple of thousand MSPs at various conferences. Paris, San Diego, Orlando, Texas, Nashville and other stops. It is a hot topic in the MSP world. I am also starting to work with MSPs to help them develop their own CoMITs practice.

---

[1] This should give you a hint about how impressive being an "Amazon Best Seller" is. Hint: Not really.

[2] Seriously, it's not a big deal. I mean, *seriously*

Yeah, I wrote it as CEO of Simplex-IT, but the message is just as valuable for any MSP with a CoMITs practice. The core concepts and requirements (it's a relationship and everybody *must* win) are going to be the same.

My last book featured Rob Rae of Datto writing an introduction. I went a little crazy in this book. Rob was gracious enough to write a piece for this one, as well. I also asked Scott Barlow over at Sophos, one of our primary cybersecurity vendors, and 3 clients at Simplex-IT.

It's great to see the whole CoMITs conversation beginning to take shape in our industry. I must point out that Rob over at Datto understood the concept almost immediately. I'm also happy to report that I'm seeing that more and more frequently with other vendors, with other MSPs, and (perhaps most importantly) potential clients.

The great thing about CoMITs is when it's done properly, everybody wins: the MSP, the client, and the Internal IT person. When the process is done poorly or forced…everybody loses.

I like these odds.

A HUGE thank you to Ann, Chris and Jerry, and all our other CoMITs clients. It is one thing for me to say this program works and has value, but your words are ten times more valuable than anything I can say.

Slightly-less-but-still-pretty-darn-big thanks to Rob and Scott. You were among the first vendor connections I made over ten years ago. You are both with different companies since then, but the relationships are still strong.

Thanks to all the MSPs that are embracing this concept. Your feedback and enthusiasm are a great reinforcement that we are building something that is pretty darn cool.

Finally, I want to thank my wife Julie for putting up with yet another off-hours project.

Introduction

I don't want your job.

Sorry to be blunt, but I wanted to start this on the right track. But maybe I need to be more specific.

I am an MSP, and I don't want your job.

Still too vague? How about:

I am an MSP Managed Service Provider, you are responsible for the IT (Information Technology) maintenance of a Small-to-Medium Business (SMB), and I don't want your job.

If you're familiar with the MSP business at all, you know that for the last 15 years or so our marketing/selling mantra was to go to your bosses and say, "We can do that better and cheaper than your employees can."

And in a lot of cases, we were right. Not always, but very often.

For the most part, the MSP industry viewed the Internal IT folks as targets. Marketing campaigns directed at attacking the internal IT folks as lacking skills, time, bandwidth, social skills, business acumen, even personal hygiene were sometimes the call of the day.

God knows there was no way we could ever work together.

Until now.

About 2 years ago we created a new service offering called "Co-Managed IT services", or *CoMITs*. It's a way to bring both parties, Internal IT folks, such as you, and the MSP, which is us, together in a partnership. Together, we can bring the strengths of both parties. Together, we can do a better job of delivering IT services to an organization than Internal IT folks or a traditional MSP relationship.

If we work together, if we trust each other, and if we take advantage of the strengths both parties bring to the table, everyone wins.

Does it work for every organization? Nope. Will it work with every form of Internal IT folk? Nope.

That's what this book is about. To talk to you, the Internal IT resource. You might be the IT Director with a small IT department. You might be the lone support resource. You might be a CIO-type manager, or you may be making it up as you go.

With CoMITs, we have your back covered, but only if you let us. Read through these pages, and we'll give you a realistic description of how we see current Internal IT support--both plusses and minuses. We will describe CoMITs to you. We will also try to help you understand whether it works for you and your organization or not.

You were probably handed this book by an MSP with whom you're considering a CoMITs relationship. They're not interested in a relationship that is forced, fake or otherwise disingenuous for either party. It just isn't worth it.

Now let me introduce you to CoMITs.

Interlude No. 1: The IT Director

When Bob first mentioned writing the forward, I thought, "Me? What do I know about writing forwards"? But then the more I thought about it, the more I thought "Why not me?". I have been working with Bob from Simplex-IT in some capacity for over the past 10 years. If I wasn't the original CoMITs Partner, long before Bob coined that actual term, I was one of the first few. I am exactly the kind of person Bob is writing this book for.

10 years ago, I was the IT person for a small business. I was overwhelmed and needed help. Then, I got a postcard from Simplex-IT. They were a local small business, and that appealed to us. We called and set an appointment to meet with them and hear their pitch. Imagine our surprise when in walked Bob. He wasn't in a suit. His curly hair needed a trim and was getting unruly. He didn't talk like an IT guy. He didn't quite act like an IT guy. But, you could tell the moment he opened his mouth that he knew what he was talking about, and he believed in what he was saying. He assured us from the very beginning that he was just there to help, not take over. Honestly, I was skeptical. I was convinced my company would see all the things Simplex-IT brought to the table and would no longer need me. I couldn't have been more wrong. I think they taught me more about my job in that first year than I care to admit.

10 years later, and I am the IT Director of a different and larger business, with a staff of IT professionals working together. Simplex-IT is still with us, now with their formal Co-Managed IT services program. It's a partnership, and a good one.

And sometimes, Bob still needs a haircut.

Ann G
IT Director, Insurance Company

Setting Expectations

WHO IS THIS BOOK WRITTEN FOR?

This book is written specifically for the individual who is responsible for the IT operations running in a small to medium business. By that, I mean you have the direct technical skills and responsibilities, you're not just working and coordinating outside vendors, acting as a conduit or lead non-technical contact.[3]

Although others (CEO, MSPs, bored lion tamers)[4] could read this and get some value, my focus is going to be on you, the IT Director. Even if you are a one-man[5] IT department. Even if you are also expected to do 20 other things altogether.

This will be especially useful for you if you, like most IT folks for SMBs, feel overwhelmed with the challenge of providing complete IT support. You're[6] asked to be an expert in Networking, Windows Active Directory, cybersecurity, Office 365, SQL Server, mobile devices, office productivity tools, end-user training, BI, the cloud, Microsoft Licensing, and quantum mechanics.[7]

---

[3] As Seinfeld would say, *"not that there's anything wrong with that"*. But, CoMITs isn't a good fit for that situation. A traditional MSP relationship, however, works great!

[4] The only way I can imagine a lion tamer being bored is because of a lack of lions. In which case, this begs the question: Are you *really* a lion tamer?

[5] Or woman. Fair warning, the gender of my pronouns or examples are going to go all over the place.

[6] I'm also going to keep things simple by referring to "you" when you might have a small department for IT support. The "You" in that case is your collective team.

[7] Of the last two, guess which one we find easier to understand?!

And often (especially in the manufacturing sector), you're asked to keep legacy (old) hardware and software working with the latest hardware and software.

We have a solution. And it works. It's not for everybody, but it works.

This book is written for Small to Medium Businesses (SMBs), because the strategy that we are proposing works best for SMB (we will explain that as we go on).

But for this to work, you need to understand the solution. You need to buy into it. Not because it's shiny, new and has a cool acronym, all of which are true, but because it makes sense for you and your organization.

In that order, yes, you come first in terms of determining whether CoMITs is good for you and your organization.

Curious? Cool.

WHAT IS THIS BOOK ABOUT?

CoMITs is an acronym for "Co-Managed IT services." It's a (quasi-) new IT (Information Technology) support model. It blends traditional "Internal IT" with traditional MSP in an extremely close partnership where both parties are committed to the success of each other.

My goal in writing this book is to give you (the Internal IT person) enough of an understanding of the CoMITs concept to decide if it *might* be a fit for you and your organization.

But before we dive into CoMITs, let's review some other terms first:

Managed Services

Managed services is the practice of outsourcing on a proactive basis certain processes and functions intended to improve operations and cut expenses.[8]

---

[8] Wikipedia: https://en.wikipedia.org/wiki/Managed_services

Companies are more and more driven to have revenue driven with a subscription model (aka "Monthly Recurring Revenue"). Less cash upfront versus a purchase, but more flexibility (and predictable cash flow) moving forward.

Managed Services (as we're using it here) is usually offered as a monthly subscription model to clients.

Notice the lack of the term IT in this definition. We are starting to see professions such as Human Resources and Accounting offered as Managed Services. We've even seen Ransomware offered as a monthly service to people who want to become malware or hacker type bad guys but are particularly lazy.

Traditionally in the IT world, the Managed Service offering is a majority (if not all) of the IT services being offered by a vendor to the client organization, usually with a fixed monthly fee. Often that monthly fee includes hardware (aka "Hardware As A Service" or HAAS), software (aka "Software As A Service" or SAAS) and licensing i.e., anti-virus and other security software, local and cloud backup, Business Continuity, and Disaster Recovery services and more.

These services are provided by the owner of the next term.

Managed Service Provider

A Managed Service Provider (or MSP) is an organization that provides…wait for it…Managed Services to their clients.

It's a compelling business model,[9] both for the client and the MSP. The client has a known budget for known services. The MSP has known cash flow and client needs. It's cheaper to prevent a problem than it is to fix it. If the MSP is proactive (which means more profitable), then the client has a healthier IT environment (more productive). Both sides win.

In a perfect world, both the client and the MSP are financially incentivized to create the best IT experience for the client.

---

[9] When it's done right

Let me know when you find that perfect world. I bet there are talking penguins there. Because that would be perfect.

Internal IT

Mmm…you. You are the employee(s)[10] whose job, primary or not, is to provide the necessary IT resources for the organization.

Don't let the traditional MSP marketing materials fool you. There is a value that you can bring to your employer that an MSP, no matter how well-meaning, can't. There are also limitations.

Usually Internal IT resources, even with the best of intentions, are overloaded in terms of expectations. There is a lot of "When you're up to your a$$ in alligators and it's hard to remember you're there to drain the swamp" that is going on there.

We will talk more about the organizational challenges of Internal IT folks later.

STMPs (Software, Tools, Methods, and Portals)

I originally introduced this term in my prior book.[11] STMPs are the Services, Tools, Methodologies, and Portals that all MSPs use in order to provide our services to our customers. It's not an MSP thing. You have your own collection of STMP's. PSA, RMM, cybersecurity tools, backup tools, monitoring, training, documentation portals, new employee onboarding checklists. All of these are examples of STMPs.

As MSP's, we're financially incentivized to develop a thorough and effective collection of STMPs. It's often difficult for Internal IT folks to get the management folks to support efforts to do the same.

---

[10] Again, I am using single person, but we could be talking about a small IT department

[11] "The MSP's Survival Guide to Co-Managed IT services". Yup, I am going to refer to it a lot. Should you read it? It certainly goes deeper into the concept, but I wouldn't consider it "required reading".

Seagulling

We love this term. Seagulling is a process where a resource comes in out of nowhere, makes a lot of noise, drops a lot of shit,[12] and flies off. I first read the term in a management book (sadly I don't recall the title, we're talking 20+ years ago). It referred to a management style. When researching my first book I realized this was also the way a lot of IT vendors approach their clients. Instead of a long-term relationship, they're there for the specific project. Or the hardware/software sale. And when they're done, they're gone. And you (the Internal IT folks) are left holding the bag.

Full of you-know-what. Yuck.

The MSP versus Internal IT:

Originally, the MSP sales model was proposed as a replacement for in house employee-based IT support. The traditional MSP model approach is usually described in this format:

MSP Salesperson: "How do you handle your IT support needs now?"

CEO: "We have an internal staff of 2 employees"

MSP Salesperson: "Oh, we can do their work better and for less. Let's get rid of them and work together!"

So, the last thing an internal IT person wanted to hear was an MSP coming in. It meant their job was in jeopardy. At the very least, the MSP was going to identify all their shortcomings.

And if the CEO protested, saying "We actually like our internal IT folks and have no intention of getting rid of them." Often, the MSP salesperson would slink away, and look for the next company to talk to.

---

[12] Sorry for the profanity, but in this case, it is appropriate.

More recently, the MSP market has matured enough so there's as often an MSP salesperson competing against an existing MSP solution.

But the Internal IT resource? It was either replace them or move on to the next potential client.

Not any longer.

To be clear, sometimes it *is* that simple as described above. Sometimes the MSP solution outperforms the internal IT department or individual.[13]

But not always. There always have been some services, some skills, some values that internal IT folks add to an organization that an MSP can't. And vice versa. More on that later.

Can't we all just get along?

That's where CoMITs comes in. We've created a strategy where a traditional MSP can partner with the internal IT folks (even it's a single individual) and provide the best of both worlds.

And. Everybody. Wins. Or. Nobody. Does.

In my previous book, "The MSP's Survival Guide to Co-Managed IT services", I described to MSPs how they can develop a successful CoMITs practice in parallel with their traditional offerings.

Now it's your turn. Now, I'm looking to describe how CoMITs might work for you, the IT Director of our potential client.

And how it can dramatically improve *your* life.

If it's right for you and your organization, that is.

And that's what this book is about, helping you understand CoMITs without a salesperson breathing down your neck. Giving you the pros and cons about the practice. CoMITs isn't for everyone.

---

[13] Looking for sugar-coating? Boy, do *you* have the wrong author.

IS THIS FOR THE CEO?

Here's the thing. In my previous CoMITs book, it took me a while to figure out how to differentiate the approach to a CEO versus an Internal IT person.

It finally hit me. It's all about ham and eggs. It's all about the classic joke:

"What is the difference between involvement and commitment? Look at a breakfast of ham and eggs. The chicken was involved, but the pig was committed."

A CEO wants the IT department to succeed. Because without it, her organization won't succeed. But for the most part, how IT succeeds isn't critical, it's more a means to an end.

But for you? This is your career, your life. You care. A lot. You are committed to the success of the IT component of the business.

To be sure, there are blurs between these lines. A successful CEO absolutely needs to know something about IT.[14] If you are going to be a truly successful Internal IT resource, you need to understand the business.[15]

So, if a CEO is reading this? Great. However, it is not written for them. This book is written for IT professionals.

It is written for You.

MY PROMISE TO YOU

Ok, let's lay our cards on the table. I am an MSP, and historically companies like mine have wanted to replace you.

Now I am knocking on your door, saying *"Trust me, we're here to help you."*

Yup, I'm sure you've heard *that* before.

---

[14] And she should read my first book, "A CEO's Survival Guide to Information Technology"

[15] More on this later.

But here's the thing. The CoMITs strategy is a complete failure if the Internal IT person fails in any way. And by failure, I mean for the MSP. Why? Because the base assumption behind CoMITs is that both parties (the MSP and the Internal IT folks) will work together to manage, maintain and improve the IT operations of their *joint customer*.

I gave one of my first presentations at an MSP conference in Nashville back in the summer of '18. I spoke directly and I thought forcefully about the need for trust between the MSP and the Internal IT staff. After the speech, another MSP came up to me and said: "Fantastic idea! And if the Internal IT folks screw up, you're right there and can take over the whole operation!"

Ah…no.

Check that.

Ah…hell, no.

Forget ethics, morality or the "Who, me? I'd never do that". How many times do we hear those type of promises, only to find the quite different truth later?

But here's the thing. As an MSP with a flourishing CoMITs practice, we are currently working to build trust with the Internal IT folks at potential customers. If we develop a reputation of using that as a wedge to get into companies and then kick the Internal folks out, how long will we be able to run this game?

If we, the MSP, play it straight? We win. We make an honest wage from an honest service.

If you, the Internal IT folks play it straight? You win. You get fantastic support from a team that knows your network, your business and knows you. We've got your back. And you've got ours.

Lastly, the client (your employer) wins. They get the benefits of both worlds. A significant cost reduction versus hiring additional staff, and higher specialized skills. Adding to this the on-premise knowledge of the business and people that only an on-site employee (you!) can bring.

I'd be stupid to mess that up. One of the most critical tools in this business in terms of developing new clients is reputation. It's easy to destroy, and very difficult to build back again. If we developed a reputation of using CoMITs to displace Internal IT folks, that's going to come back to haunt us big time.

I'm stupid, but not *that* stupid.

What's the promise?

Sorry, I got distracted. CoMITs isn't for everybody. There are MSP's that shouldn't do it, like the example I mentioned above. And there are organizations that shouldn't bring a CoMITs MSP relationship in-house, and we'll get into that later.

I'm going to give you a straight description of the CoMITs methodology from the Internal IT perspective. Good and bad. ***I'm going to explain when you shouldn't go CoMITs.***** There are some situations that simply won't work.

I promise.

Why should you trust me?

Implementing a bad CoMITs environment is costly. Nobody benefits. Everybody loses.

So, if you're looking for one of those books where the main topic is the latest shiny thing that will solve all woes, keep looking.

Let me know if you find it.

Interlude No. 2:
The MSP Services Vendor

We are all under attack. These days, hackers are smarter, faster and better funded than at any other point in IT history. Why? Money. Hacking used to be more of an annoyance however now it's been commoditized. Theft of information sold and auctioned on the dark web and malware like ransomware has made the business of hacking a lucrative profession. Traditional technologies aren't keeping up, which has led to a flood of newer software and hardware vendors entering the market more so than ever before, all to stay one step ahead of the bad guys.

With newer technologies like cloud and IoT (Internet of Things), this has led to more entryways for black hats. We have seen thousands of credit card numbers stolen from large businesses because of an HVAC system. We have seen ransomware spread because of something as simple as not implementing two-factor authentication (2FA or MFA) and poor password management leading to millions of dollars in lost downtime. It's nearly impossible for any of us to stay on top of our world as IT changes minute by minute.

When something bad does happen, who's to blame? The IT guys. A recent ransomware attack of a city in Florida cost the business millions of dollars and the in-house IT guy his job. He wasn't the cause of the attack; but in their mind, he should have been better prepared. With everything you must focus on, how can you properly manage it all? This is where the Managed Service Provider (MSP) comes in to play.

Yes, it is true that MSPs have been selling a complete IT outsourced solution for decades now to small and medium-sized businesses however there is a massive opportunity for both the end-user and this channel of IT pros to work together.

Because the MSP focuses solely on IT and more so IT security, they are very knowledgeable of these current threats. MSPs have had the time to find, vet and build better security options which means that we are at a stage where a small business with no in house IT guys and much smaller budgets can have better IT security than mid and large market companies do. But it's much more than technology. It's education, experience and let's face it, it's hard to find good IT talent these days.

You bring value as well. You know your company. You know the users, the value that IT can bring on a day to day value. You are able to bring this value more directly and more efficiently than any MSP can.

That is where CoMITs comes into the picture, taking the best of both worlds and creating a relationship-based process.

Bob carefully goes through how this is not an outsourced play. This is a very good complement to your current IT plan. What can be gained by working together is efficiency, knowledge, and peace of mind for all of us, all at a very affordable cost.

Rob Rae
VP of Business Development
Datto Inc.

Players and Playground

INTRODUCTION

Sorry, but I am going to get in trouble here. Most IT organizations in the SMB market have weaknesses. I mean, honestly, how could they not? They all have a small IT staff. In many cases, they have just one employee. How are you supposed to keep up with all the advancements? The latest cybersecurity issues? Managing backups? Database issues? BI opportunities? Cloud? Virtualization? Documentation? Training end-users? IT planning? Resetting the %!@#$# android phone for the CEO's son for the 99th time, whose sole goal in life is to download all that is downloadable?

I need to make something clear here. We worked with about 20-30 internal IT "departments" over the past dozen or so years on some level of CoMITs, pre-dating the official creation of the term. And you can honestly add another near-hundred or so companies that over the many, many, many years[16] I have worked with as consultant, CIO, IT Director or other roles. We've seen many levels of competency, quality, engagement, morale, pride, depression, and various other adjectives. Somewhere it was a wonder that electrical current still flowed, let alone data, and others. And others where there was an incredible level of quality provided by fantastic employees, who were often taken for granted by management.

---

[16] Seriously, I'm old. The word "Crotchety" might get the attention, but "old" is there for a reason.

TRADITIONAL IT SUPPORT MODELS[17]

Here are what I consider to be the five standard Support Models for the traditional SMB organization. I'm going to try to present each model equally, not skew the perspective in favor of one direction or another. A well-implemented model will usually beat out a poorly implemented model, regardless of other factors.

The five models are:

- **Seagull Vendors:** No real internal resources for IT. A relationship with a vendor who will act like a seagull ("come in out of nowhere, make a lot of noise, drop a lot of shit, and then fly off"). Ok, I'm failing miserably at presenting each model equally. It's my book. Deal with it.
- **Internal IT:** As we discussed, an individual or group of individuals who have the responsibility of dealing with the IT needs of the organization. Vendors may be brought in occasionally but under the control and direction of the Internal IT staff.
- **Silo Support:** This is where a vendor is engaged to give support on one single aspect of an organization's IT, with strict borders as to where responsibilities begin and end. Some common examples are security, backups, firewalls, and database (i.e., SQL/Oracle).
- **Managed Services:** An external organization that provides IT services to the organization, usually through a monthly/annual contract with some fixed fee. In other words, me<g>.
- **CoMITs:** Co-Managed IT services. The combination of two of the three above options. I'll leave it to you to determine which two of the three. (Hint: neither involves birds.)

---

[17] Some of this is directly from my "The MSP's Survival Guide to Co-Managed IT services" book.

Seagull Vendors	
Benefits	
Cost	The only time you need to pay someone is when you bring in the seagull. You're only paying someone for the project/purchase/service at hand.
Expertise	If you're selecting your seagull properly, then they have the expertise to do what you need them to do.
Risks	
No Focus	The only time these people are involved is when you call them. No preventative work, no proactive work.
No Incentive	The Seagull's priorities, even with the best of intentions is cash flow. All discussions will center around billable time and selling products. Even the most honest of them have a bottom line to work around.
Continuity	There's no strategic plan. Just reacting to the situation and current need.
Cost	The idea of seagulls being cheaper is making the critical error of treating IT as a Cost Center. That really wasn't smart even in the 20th Century.

Internal IT	
Benefits	
Control	All facets of the department whether one person or many, are under the control of the organization. This is a double-edged sword, but it can be beneficial.
Prioritization	No other organization has greater priority for the IT resources.
Focus	The company is always the focus.

| Understanding | Business Critical services, products, offerings are well understood by the IT staff, as long as there is mutual understanding between the IT folks and management. |
| Unique IT Requirements | If the organization has unique IT requirements, the IT staff can be well-versed on them. |

Risks

Stifle Growth	If there is no external input or connection, then opportunities to improve the impact of IT on the organization is lost. In 2018 we were talking to several companies still running Windows Server 2003 because it "still works."
Self-Taught	Often with single person IT departments, little or no priority is given to learning new skills or tools. And best practices are rare. In most cases, many home-grown standards are implemented.
Skills	Most people working in small IT departments must wear several hats. So, the skill sets are spread out over several technologies. This leaves special skills (i.e., security, SQL, Active Directory) to be somewhat lacking.
Turnover	A person leaving the department, especially from a single person department can be very disruptive.
Absence	A person going on vacation can be traumatic.

Silo Support	
Benefits	
Easy to replace	Because they're very specific, they should be able to be surgically removed and replaced.
Non-invasive	They should not interfere with your day to day operations.
Expertise	You are paying for specific expertise and only that expertise.

Risks	
Finger Pointing	If they don't understand how their silo integrates with other aspects of your organization, several square peg and round hole situations can arise.
No integration	Silos usually don't pay attention to other areas of the organization to look for best practices or opportunities except as predators/hunters.
Faceless	Greater chance for miscommunication. Silo services are often presented as commodities, resulting in cookie-cutter service delivery.

Traditional MSP	
Benefits	
Cost	A good MSP *should* be less expensive than a similarly skilled[18] internal IT department with traditional IT needs.
Technical Pool	MSPs have a larger technical pool from which to draw from. That means minimal difficulty getting a technician with the appropriate skill set to attend to an issue requiring that skill set.
Strategic IT Insight	A good MSP can talk tactically and yet think strategically.
Virtual CIO[19]	A good MSP can offer "virtual CIO" services and help make sure that the business needs of the organization are well handled by the IT process and vice versa.

---

[18] Assuming it's a fair apple to apples comparison. MSPs can easily offer things like Policies and Procedures, Cyber Security Training, 24/7 coverage, and specialized skills that internal IT departments in SMBs don't have the depth to research and offer.

[19] CIO: Chief Information Officer. Also known as CTO: Chief Technology Officer.

| Low Hanging IT Requirements | Many IT needs are ignored by internal IT departments because they don't have the time (or priority) to research. The MSP can include these things in their offerings because they have already done the research. Examples include documentation, training, standards and more. |
| Up to Date | MSPs have a vested interest in keeping up with technologies and keeping their skill sets and offerings current. |

Risks

Not all MSPs created equal	Sturgeon's[20] Law: "Ninety percent of everything is crap" is true in most cases in life. Not all MSPs are created equal. Especially disconcerting are MSPs that totally focus on monitoring and troubleshooting devices only.
Long Contracts	Many MSPs require long-term agreements with their customers that are hard to get out of. Though this method is starting to fade away in recent years.
Skill	Thanks to Sturgeon, not all MSPs have or maintain their skill set.
Customer Unique Expertise	If a customer has a unique IT requirement, the only incentive the MSP must learn it is for that customer. So, the MSP will look to pass all costs of developing that skill on to that single customer.
Culture Integration	Boy, if the culture of an MSP does not match the culture of the customer at least to some degree, it isn't going to work. This is doubly true in the CoMITs world.

---

[20] Theodore Sturgeon: Science Fiction Author and critic.

Co-Managed IT Services	
Benefits	
Best of both worlds	A good CoMITs agreement should utilize the strengths of both Internal IT and MSP models, and create a "glue" between them.
Internal and External Views	Internal resources understand the internals better. External resources (MSP) understand the IT world better. Combined? That's potential for very good mojo.
On-Site Focus	The on-site resources can focus their attention and resources to get the best bang for the buck.
Risks	
Poor Communication	If there isn't a good amount of communication, it's going to go poorly.
Finger Pointing	If blame is a popular diagnostic tool for either party, this is going to go poorly.
Potentially Disjointed	If internal IT refuses to use tools or accept best practices, friction occurs.
Inflexible MSP	If the MSP comes in from on high with a "We will show you the right way to do things, and it's our way" without regard to your world, it's a takeover, not a cooperative relationship.
Inflexible Internal IT	What's good for the goose… If you as an Internal IT refuse to consider seriously another opinion or approach to your IT support model, we have a problem. Especially when it comes to handling traditional IT issues, not requirements driven by unique business requirements. Again, not a cooperative relationship.
Management Interference	If management wants to use CoMITs to sabotage their Internal IT,[21] all parties will suffer.
Growing Pains	The first few customers that an MSP implements this model will be…interesting.

YOUR WORLD: INTERNAL IT FOR THE SMB

Introduction

Being part of an SMB brings challenges as well as opportunities. But the complexity of IT, both in terms of opportunity and risk, can't be fully handled by one or two IT people. To be clear, this isn't a slam on you. Nor is it an attempt to say "Oh, your network is going to crash and it's all your fault if you don't buy into the CoMITs model immediately!"

The IT department for the average SMB is often understaffed and under budget. You can handle the day to day operations, but not upgrades or significant incidents. You must remember ancient technology as the shop floor stuff only works with XP and would cost $150,000 to replace, with no time to learn anything new.

Let's review some common challenges for the SMB IT folks, as well as some common organizational structures.

IT Challenges for SMBs

But almost by definition, the IT resources for the SMB are restricted, especially in terms of bodies. Let's categorize some of these restrictions:

IT Challenges for SMB's	
Limitation	**Description**
Situational Bandwidth	Those special times where you need additional bodies, but only for a short period of time.
IT Specialization	The difference between Operational and Advanced Skill. For example, it's one thing to keep a SQL database running, another to troubleshoot performance.
IT Best Practices	Developing and maintaining standard best practices for common actions (onboarding/offboarding employees, backup strategies, etc.

IT Challenges for SMB's	
Limitation	**Description**
STMP's	Evaluation, Implementation, Maintenance of the tools that maximize the productivity of the IT department.
Keeping Up	It's important to know what's happening in the IT world.
Irreplaceability	The smaller the department, the harder it is to take a vacation. Or lunch.
Vertical Specialization	What makes the organization special to the SMB's clients? How to use IT to maximize that value?[22]

The Seagull Dilemma

The most common solution for SMB's with a skills gap is the Seagull. Bringing in a vendor who can fill in the gap, you only pay for what you need, right? Makes sense. Bodies (bandwidth), skills specialization, and so on. In my prior lives as IT Director and CIO, I have brought in my share of Seagulls over the years. And as a consultant to 40–50 organizations throughout my career, I have been a Seagull as well.

A great vendor relationship is definitely possible. But there are inherent challenges and limitations.

The challenge is in the term Seagull. The vendor doesn't have operational eyes on your organization (whether specific to IT or in general) unless there is an ongoing relationship. And often they'll come in with an attitude of "Absolutely, we can solve your problem! Ummmm…by the way, what's your problem?"

---

[22] IMHO, this one is where the internal IT value is greatest, hardest to outsource, and least utilized. More on that later.

Seagull Challenges	
Limitation	**Description**
Disconnect	Without an ongoing relationship, how well do they know the needs and goals of your organization?
No Skills Transfer	Often the work of seagulls doesn't include enough skills transfer
Seagull de jour	The vendor selection process, repeatedly.
Learning Curves	Especially true when the vendors change frequently.
Strategic vs Tactical	Vendors coming in with their solution to the immediate, specified problem. Tactically great, but does it fit into the strategic needs of the organization?
Abandonment	When they're done, so is their revenue stream. So additional support can be spotty.
Price before Value	SMB management often has a focus on price. It's often hard to justify longer-term value in IT projects to non-IT folks.
Everything is a Sales Pitch[23]	The vendor is there to sell. And sell.

One final note here. Absolutely, there are great vendor relationships. You probably already have a couple. It's my belief that a majority of vendors truly do wish the best for their clients and trust their solutions as they are presenting them.

I am just saying that there is a way to get the best of all worlds if everybody is on the same page.

---

[23] The biggest challenge. Are they proposing a solution because of their sales quota? Or it's their favorite technology?

Common Internal IT Configurations

Internal IT organizations can take several shapes. Here are exaggerated examples of ones we have seen and worked with most often:

1. **One Man Shop.** The most common. We see it a lot in small- medium manufacturing companies especially older ones. There is a single person wearing all the IT hats. Often a low person on the totem pole overwhelmed and feeling unloved.

2. **Batman/Robin.** This is a 2 (possibly 3) person IT shop. One person is clearly the senior tech whether by title or just skill level and does the "heavy lifting" in terms of advanced work. The second person is the junior, often delegated to desktop only. Very little skill-sharing since there is no time to teach.

3. **Monitoring Only.** A popular option for MSPs about 5–10 years ago. The idea was to use the monitoring RMM tools for the client, but not include any actual remedial or proactive work as part of the monthly fee. That costs extra. This is not CoMITs.

4. **Missing Skills/Vertical.** We've run into this several times, especially with database/BI work (SQL, Oracle). In these cases, we were close to a silo MSP as mentioned before, but we try to share additional tools outside our silo.

5. **Wasted Value.** Their current IT staff has skills outside of traditional IT that make them much more profitable, but they never have the time because the more mundane IT issues keep pulling them away. We have heard the statement "We could bill Sarah's time to a client at $175 an hour but she had to help an end-user with a PowerPoint problem."[24]

---

[24] Again, the biggest opportunity for both the SMB and the internal IT folks

ARE YOU A CIO?

CIOs (Chief Information Officer) and CTOs (Chief Technology Officer) are cool. By far and away, they're the coolest jobs on the planet. They make tons of money, fly around in jet packs, defeat super villains and never get their hair mussed doing it.

And then I wake up.

Wikipedia defines the CIO: *"Chief Information Officer (CIO), Chief Digital Information Officer (CDIO) or Information Technology (IT) Director, is a job title commonly given to the most senior executive in an enterprise who works with information technology and computer systems in order to support enterprise goals."*

Yup. Head geek. I don't want to get into the discussion of the title itself. IMHO, that's as much a political issue as anything else. But the bottom line is the CIO holds a strategic role in terms of the future of the organization. Notice I didn't say anything about tech in that statement.

A good percentage of organizations hold IT at arm's length in terms of planning for the future. Almost a necessary evil, or just a cost of doing business. In my experience, this is often a subset of the age of management and how embracing they are of the 21st Century.

With these types of organizations, IT rarely gets asked to join in any reindeer games. When significant changes to the organizations are considered, the tech side of it is either ignored or there's a vendor from the outside bringing it in without regard to the status quo (including you!). Upgrades are done when stuff quits working. And nothing strikes fear in the heart of the ignored IT staff than the CEO saying "Hey, I read something the other day…".

My favorite is situations where internal IT has been saying something to management for years only to be ignored. A consultant comes in and says the same thing and it's treated as gospel.

Not with a CoMITs type of situation.[25]

With a CoMITs situation, you know the goals and objectives of the organization, and even have a voice in the process. We work together to know that we both have a voice. You know the impact IT has on the organization, and work with the rest of management to find ways to improve that impact. You can make sure that the newest trends in IT can be harnessed appropriately both for current and future needs.

The key thing is you understand the business. And the business understands IT.

That's hard to do in an understaffed, overwhelmed traditional SMB IT department. Especially when you don't have the management or CIO experience. And bringing in a consultant/vendor/seagull to help you with that? Either it's going to be quick (a 1-day seminar?), or expensive long-term coaching.

You need some time in your schedule. Someone to talk to who understands your business and the CIO role and isn't going anywhere. And someone who can back you up in the process.

And *maybe*...just **maybe**...there's a jet pack in your future.

WHAT DO YOU WANT TO BE WHEN YOU GROW UP?

Growing up seems to be a lot of work. I'm still not 100% sure when I am going to get around to it.

That said, professional development is critical these days. Especially if you are in the IT business. A friend of mine once told me back in the early 90s that the definition of obsolescence in IT is "does it work?". And I think there is still some truth in that. By and large, our industry reinvents the core technology over the span of 5-10 years. This means that you will need to reinvent your skills constantly or stay at a company that's stagnant from a technology perspective. And hope you can stay there for a long, long time, until.

---

[25] I'm not talking title. I'm talking about how the position related within the organization. I'm not a big title guy.

Until the organization decides that IT needs to be completely replaced. Often starting with you. This is a bleak future for you, I'm afraid.

Honestly, the future isn't much better for organizations that don't change with the times. By sticking with the older technologies, companies are also ignoring the opportunities that the newer technologies bring. We are all seeing tremendous flexibility in terms of product offering, marketing, customer services, vendor relations, and employee productivity and collaboration. These are all results of newer technology being used appropriately.

Don't get me started about the vulnerability of old technology that still faces the outside world in some capacity. Seriously. Don't get me started. It's not pretty.

You can't do that with servers that are almost teenagers.

The question is, where do you see yourself improving in terms of professional skills in the next 5 years? What are you doing to achieve that improvement? If you are dependent on the seagulls, you're not going to improve there. Google is great for individual items. Classes are expensive, and usually only partially applicable.

It would be cool if you had a partnership that helped you learn almost casually on your equipment while working with your organization.

Working with *you*.

Ready to see something that might be that cool?

Interlude No. 3:
The Network Administrator

I've been working with Bob and Simplex-IT for over a decade now. Things started off on a small scale and quickly grew when we realized as an IT staff that we needed support. Around the time of the economic downturn in 2007, our company began to restructure the IT staff. That meant I was about to be responsible for what at one time 4 people covered. Everything from learning the ERP system, maintaining the IT infrastructure, SQL, Exchange Server, you name it and I was having to deal with it. That's where managed IT comes in to play.

I often wondered if the trend would be to do away with onsite IT support. Looking back, I think that may have affected my attitude towards any Managed IT I would be dealing with. But when Bob started talking to me about Co-Managed IT support, I bought in 100%. It's exactly the model that our type of IT organization needs. I would like to add that Simplex-IT has been talking to me about this business model for a while now, so it's not new to either of us.

As the years progressed, and the relationships grew I felt more and more comfortable collaborating with them. The folks at Simplex-IT make "**IT**" fun. They have a great sense of humor, and they are serious when it comes down to business. We all know how stressful things can get, and they know how to balance that dynamic. I think that it's genuine and it shows. That's what makes relationships grow and succeed.

It comes down to mutual respect and a desire to solve problems to make life easier. Another way to describe a CoMITs relationship is that they are a sort of hybrid IT staff. It allows us to utilize the tools and experience that Simplex-IT has that we wouldn't normally have access to. We also act as a resource for them, since we have a better understanding of the business due to our experience at the company. That means we can provide Simplex-IT with details in relation to our business. The information we share with them enables the support staff to more efficiently support our users when it is needed. That's what it really comes down to is giving the best possible service to our users and/or customers.

I feel confident moving forward that our IT staff will be better equipped to deal with issues as they arise. On this path, I can see us continuing to grow and get more efficient as time goes on. I consider Simplex-IT more of a partner than a Customer-Vendor relationship. That is a key mindset for the CoMITs strategy.

Chris K
Network Administrator
Manufacturing Company

CoMITs

INTRODUCTION[26]

Co-Managed IT services (CoMITs) is a hybrid relationship between the Internal IT resources and the MSP provider. CoMITs creates a partnership between you and the MSP. It truly is a partnership, or else it will fail. Plain and simple.

Primarily, it's about the Services, Tools, Methodologies, and Portals (or STMPs). These are products that all us MSPs use in order to provide our services to you, our customers.

We segment our IT responsibilities. Using our STMPs, you'll be responsible for supporting some (or all) of the IT resources for your organization. And we're (the MSP) responsible for the rest. A common example would be the MSP takes care of the servers and infrastructure, and you're responsible for end-users and desktops (or vice versa).[27]

We then actively encourage you to fully use our STMPs. Whatever PSA, RMM, cybersecurity tools, backup tools, monitoring, training, documentation portal…we give you whatever access we can for you to do your job.

If you just need some advice on an issue, want to run something by us? No problem, and no charge. We're here to help. Free advice. If you'd rather, you can escalate the issue to us.[28]

---

[26] There's a lot of information that's reworded from "The MSP's Survival Guide…" In fact, if you're bored you should read it and see how I'm saying the exact same thing, but from the MSP's perspective.

[27] We will explain the 3 most common scenarios we've seen later.

[28] For an additional charge.

And we train you. We support you. We point out shortcomings in our tools and how to get around them. Your success is our success.

It is that simple. At least the concept is. Think of it in terms of the following steps:

- Define what layers of IT are covered by you and what will be covered by the MSP[29]
- "Lift up" your IT support operations and slide all our STMPs underneath you for *all* IT layers.
- We provide training and support for the STMPs to you.
- If you need help or advice on uncovered items, the MSP will provide that freely and openly.
- You can easily escalate a ticket/project/issue to us, who will handle the issue for additional T&M charges.
- Build a relationship based on cooperation and trust between both parties.

Important Note #1:

If you can't treat a CoMITs relationship as a mutually supporting arrangement between you and the MSP, then CoMITs, or at least my version of it isn't for you. Thanks for reading the book, though.

USING OUR STMPS:

For each of these CoMITs solutions, we try to include as many services as are appropriate to the customer, even if they aren't part of our focus. We offer any of our STMPs and encourage you to embrace and use them fully. These can include (listed in alphabetical order):

---

[29] See "Common Configurations" coming up in a couple of pages.

Type of STMP

Advanced endpoint (server and workstation)

Backup/Business Continuity/Disaster Recovery

Cloud Services Management

Cyber Security Training, IT Policies, and Procedures

Dark Web Monitoring

Documentation for both customer and MSP

End-User training

Firewall/Unified Threat Management device

Invoice/Payment Portal

IT ticketing system

Malware tool

Network Reporting

Password Management

PSA (Professional Services Automation) Tool

RMM (Remote Monitoring and Management) Tool

Screen Control/end-user support tool

SNMP (non-Windows) based network monitoring

Spam filter

Web filtering

Not all these products will be used for every client. There are also other products that we didn't include (specialty products for SQL, or VOIP technologies) to keep things quasi-simple.

The point is that we try to include as many of these tools as are appropriate in our CoMITs offering and encourage and support the Internal IT Folks to use these STMPs in their daily routines.

Think about it. We have evaluated all these STMPs across all our clients. We know how they work. The shortcuts. The best practices. When it's time to upgrade them, or even replace them, it will happen without you breaking a sweat.

You don't have to go through near as rigorous an evaluation process, since we already have (after all, we must provide solutions that will work for all our clients. Nor, do you have to learn how to implement and configure any new product. That's our (the MSP) job.

HOW DOES IT WORK?

Using the STMPs provided by the MSP (us), you'll be able to proactively monitor and manage all the IT resources within your organization. In the case of split responsibilities, the MSP manages the resources they are responsible for. The monitoring services may generate alerts that create tickets in the PSA system. So may users.[30] These tickets are ways to track actions and solutions. Both you and the MSP will track activities using these tickets. These tickets then go through a process (as seen in the diagram below).

---

[30] Pesky buggers.

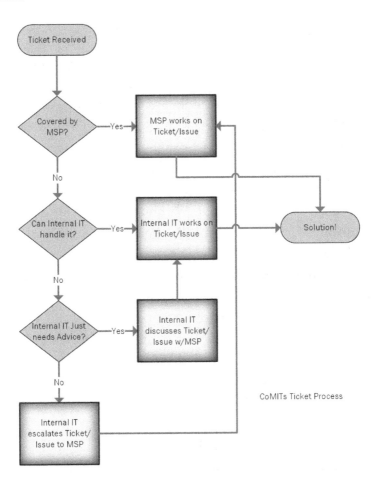

CoMITs Ticket Process

It's simple. The PSA will evaluate the ticket and forward it to the appropriate party. If the ticket is an issue covered by the MSP,[31] then the MSP handles the issue. If not, the ticket goes to you. If you need advice, just contact the MSP. Either way, you handle the ticket and update it accordingly.

If you'd rather the MSP handle the ticket, simply escalate the ticket. Then the MSP will be responsible. This is the only situation where you would incur additional costs from the monthly MSP fee (in terms of tickets).

---

[31] We'll talk about split coverage later. And "Splitsville", for which I apologize in advance.

IT'S ALL ABOUT THE RELATIONSHIP

To be blunt, I'm using a decent amount of materials from my original CoMITs book for this one. Why? First, I'm lazy. I mean, seriously lazy. But really, the books are focused on the exact same topic. My first book from the provider (MSP) point of view. This book from the consumer (you).

Anyhow, it's interesting that I use the word "Relationship" 65 times in my prior book.[32] Because it's absolutely a critical aspect of the CoMITs concept. Without a strong and supportive relationship, CoMITs will fail. For both parties. Nobody walks away from a winner.

This is critical to understand, especially in the beginning. Let's face it, the original MSP concept was created as a great way to minimize IT cost and improve the service for an organization, and a big part of the savings was achieved by eliminating you. For years, that was our pitch. We the MSP can do it better and cheaper than you, the Internal IT folks.

Now I'm talking about how we can do a better job…together?

In a word, yes. In other words…hybrid.

Let's face it, there are some benefits that Internal IT folks bring that an MSP, even with the best of intentions can't touch.

If the Internal IT folks are properly trained, supported, motivated and directed.

You'll have a better handle on internal priorities. Special needs for unique requirements. Older applications and equipment. Soft skills, dealing with "unique" users. The MSP, despite our claims, can't do that as effectively as you can. Especially in the SMB space.

And there are some benefits that the MSP brings that the Internal IT folks, even with the best of intentions can't touch.

---

[32] For those interested I only use "Relationship" 39 times in this book. But it's a shorter book. Wait…40 times.

If the MSPs resources are properly trained, supported, motivated and directed.

We have a better handle on industry trends. We have more automated tools and better-defined best practices. We don't have skills that only one person understands. We're constantly looking to improve our tools and improve the base services that we offer. We can add additional resources and special skills equal to specific situations. The Internal IT folks, despite best intentions, can't do that as effectively as we can. Especially in the SMB space.

Take both of those statements with grains of salt. I'm comparing both parties (you and the MSP) as if they're both equally well-prepared for the work.

A Good Internal IT staff will outperform a Bad MSP. And vice versa.

My point is this:. In a CoMITs relationship, the Internal IT folks are enhanced through the support of the MSP. Our success is equally measured by the improvement of Internal IT as it is by the increased productivity of the client organization.

The next couple of shaded sections are lifted from my "The MSP's Survival Guide to Co-Managed IT services" book.

Is CoMITs for you and your organization?[33]

First, are you already doing it? As I mentioned before, I've spoken with several MSPs who confessed to already have a client that has an internal IT department, and "We just worked something out between us" without giving it a name. The question is, can you formalize it and integrate it into your marketing, sales and service delivery process? You probably can, although you might need to change things a bit (so you can easily duplicate it to other customers).

---

[33] Remember, for this section I'm "speaking" to the MSP. You're technically eavesdropping<g>. And I've omitted a couple of points included here that I've made already elsewhere in this book.

Second, are you willing to give up the levels of control and transparency necessary to partner with another IT entity to the level necessary? We're talking about:

1. **Partnership.** This must be a partnership. Not between you and the customer organization (hopefully you're already on board with that or you're in trouble, my friend<g>). I'm talking about the partnership between the IT department of your customer and your organization. You need to be looking at their success as you would your own success.

2. **Flexibility.** You must be willing to change your approach to better integrate with the IT department of your customers. But not too much, and for the right reason. If you come in with the attitude of everything you do is perfect, therefore the customer IT department will, of course, accept all suggestions and new procedures without question…you'll have problems.

3. **Openness.** Transparency is king. All your cards on the table. All monitoring tools shared with your customer. Obviously different credentials, but you must make them part of your group, and vice versa.

4. **Make them look better.** I *Can't* stress this enough. Your goal is to make the internal IT department look better. Give them credit for good performance, or at the very least share credit with them. Never give them a reason to distrust you.

5. **You've got their back.** You want the IT department to thank their lucky stars that you came on board. Not that management brought you in because they don't trust you. Not that you're looking for ways to take their job.

This happened once with us besides from the earlier example. A customer of ours was very dissatisfied with their IT staff, literally one guy. And we added monitoring and worked with their IT guy. And boy he was a jerk. Blamed everything on the users. Refused to replace an obviously bad keyboard because according to him the user "would just break this one." I wish I was kidding. The epitome of all IT tech stereotypes.

I mean, the guy was a jerk.

I worked with the CEO for about six months around this guy and the CEO was and still is a tremendously nice gentleman. I had a heart to heart conversations with the IT guy. He talked about how the employees were "his customers" and all that jargon.

I never discussed and honestly never thought about taking the guy's job.

Now, to be clear, the guy should have been fired. Way early on, but the CEO didn't want to fire him.

He was finally let go with a ridiculous parachute.

Only then did I discuss with the CEO about our services moving forward.

The result? Probably not what you're thinking, they decided quite properly, in my humble opinion to hire another, more experienced IT employee and we helped with the interviewing and hiring process.

Since then, they're one of our first CoMITs customers and one of our biggest fans.

What kind of customer is a good fit for CoMITs?

Here are my thoughts on this. Don't take this as absolute gospel. There are subtle nuances beyond this list that can make a potential customer a better (or worse) CoMITs opportunity. But I think this is a good starting point:

1. The organization already has an internal IT department or in-dividual.
2. The organization sees value in having "good IT."
3. The organization sees value in or just likes their Internal IT Resource.

4. The Internal IT Resource has significant shortcomings that can be addressed with a CoMITs solution.

5. The Internal IT Resource is open to building a close relationship with a CoMITs provider.

YOU BECOME AN EXTENSION OF THE MSP

The best CoMITs relationships (IMHO) come from a significant amount of integration between both parties as a normal day to day operations. And by that, I don't necessarily mean daily chats, formal communications or red tape bureaucratic pieces, long walks on the beach, or that sort of thing.

I mean that the Internal IT folks are really using the STMPs provided by the MSP as effectively and efficiently as the MSP's technicians do. The only exceptions would be where the client is better served *in the long run*[34] by doing something different and unique.

Why? Because the MSP has had more resources dedicated to finding the "best" combinations of STMPs. They've had more time to determine the "best implementation" of the STMPs. They had more time to create the "best practices" of their STMPs. They created the most efficient pieces of automation for the STMPs.

When you want to ask for help and advice, if you are both looking at things from the same perspective and using the same STMPs, you have minimized the amount of conversation needed to get everybody on the same page.

You are all reading from the same book. Singing from the same hymnal. Swimming in the same pond. Dancing to the same song. Kissing the same frog. Watching the same Star Trek. Appreciating the same Sherlock Holmes.[35]

---

[34] We'll discuss why the italicized in the long run in a bit

[35] The best of whom is Jeremy Brett, as I pointed out in "A CEO's Survival Guide to Information Technology". No contest.

BUT I ALREADY HAVE SOME STMPS!

This happens frequently. You already have some of the STMPs that the MSP is offering. So, why abandon those to go with the ST-MPs of the MSP? In most cases, the objection isn't about the quality of the new STMP, it's the cost.

Here's the problem. The MSP probably is using its STMP across its entire client base. Literally dozens of other organizations. They have probably spent more time evaluating the STMP than you did, and they certainly know the STMP better than they know yours.

I dare say the MSP, obviously not always knows how to use their STMP better than you know how to use yours.

Here's the risk. By sticking with your STMP, you will make the MSP less effective in supporting it or increase the cost by introducing a learning curve. Either way, your short-term savings go away in the long term.

The exception to this would be where an STMP is adding specific value to your organization that the MSP-offered STMP can't. If that's the case, then the STMP should be maintained, but somewhere the cost and responsibility of supporting that STMP needs to be addressed.

Notice that I'm not explicitly telling you whether you should keep your existing STMPs or not. I'm simply stating that keeping an existing STMP that the MSP isn't familiar with decreases the immediate value of the MSP's knowledge without the MSP investing time to develop a skill set into your specific STMP.

THE MSP BECOMES AN EXTENSION OF YOU

This relationship goes both ways. It *must* be in order to work.

You bring specific value to your organization. I'm right, aren't I?[36] You understand the business needs better. You have a positive relationship

---

[36] If you don't, then now's the time to start thinking about changing that. Because the next MSP to reach out to your CEO probably won't be talking about CoMITs.

with the end-users. You're physically there. You understand the legacy applications and equipment.

By sharing that with the MSP, they'll be able to improve their productivity because there is no efficient way they can learn that stuff without you. They need you and need your cooperation.

However, if you share that information and resource with the MSP, won't you lose your advantage? Won't they then be able to walk in and replace you?

Whoa, maybe that has been their intention from the beginning! Learn your secrets with all this CoMITs talk, then swoop in and take your job!

I get that. As I mentioned in the book excerpt earlier, I've had MSPs come up to me and think that would be a great side-benefit from the CoMITs concept.

Think that through. We're spending a lot of money and time[37] creating this program.

Most MSPs including us, primarily work in a specific geographical area. If word gets out and of course it would, that we were using CoMITs as a sneaky way to unseat internal IT folks, our reputation is dead.

A great reputation takes years to rebuild if it can be rebuilt at all.

From the MSP's perspective, there is money to be made by delivering this product as is, with full honesty and the best intentions and goals for all concerned. To approach it in any other way is at best short-term gains with a dead-end future.

Forget about honesty and truthfulness. I want this investment to *keep* paying off.

With CoMITs, we're in this together, or not at all.

---

[37] I mean 2 books for crying out loud!

AT THE HEART OF COMITS

People love options. They hate decisions.

One of the strengths of CoMITs is the flexibility it brings to all parties. We're looking to create a relationship where:

All IT Responsibilities = Internal IT Responsibilities + CoMITs Provider Responsibilities

We want you to use our STMPs[38] whenever possible. In other words, we want you to be as much of an extension of our organization as we are of yours.

But let's take a moment to discuss what we mean by split. Again, like many other CoMITs topics, your mileage may vary. But the model is straightforward:

1. The CoMITs agreement will provide all the tools necessary to manage and monitor the IT resources of your organization.
2. You (the Internal IT folks) will manage a subset of the IT resources using the MSP's STMPs., based on your skills and priorities).
3. We will manage the remaining IT resources.[39]
4. For the IT resources, you are responsible for, you can ask for advice, run something by us, perform sanity checks *without any additional charge.*
5. If you want us to fully handle a ticket/situation that you are responsible for, you can simply escalate it to us, and we'll take care of it (for an additional cost).[40]

---

[38] Services, Tools, Methodologies and Portals

[39] In some cases, this subset is empty. In other words, the MSP is fully responsible for nothing. Don't mistake this for a monitoring only contract. It isn't, because you're also providing all the STMPs to the Internal IT Folks.

[40] And you can ask to "watch" us handle it or refer to the ticketing documentation, so you won't have to ask us again, if you'd like. No secrets here!

IT'S "SPLITSVILLE", BABY!

To be honest, I have no idea what brain cells were firing when I came up with the concept of "Splitsville". If you're reading this, apparently it survived to the actual publishing of the book. My apologies.

That said, the concept of the split is important. At the heart of the matter is determining where you, the Internal IT resource need the MSPs resources most. And by resources, I'm not talking about the STMPs. Those are (in most cases) across the entire IT landscape.

The question is where do you want to be primarily responsible versus the MSP? Think of it in terms of your IT falls under 2 categories:

You can do it. You have the skills, resources and time (especially armed with the STMPs) to support this layer of technology.

We (the MSP) can do it. You're expecting the MSP to automatically take the lead on these items.

The idea is straightforward. STMPs, for the most part, generate alerts, which often can become tickets. Same thing for users.

By categorizing the responsibility to either you or the MSP, we can control the flow of information, alerts, submitted user issues and more to the appropriate party.

As you can see, the more resources that fall to the MSP, the higher the agreement monthly fees. The more they fall to you, the lower.

Pretty simple.

FLAVORS OF COMITS

The question is, where's the split? Here are the 3 most common CoMITs "configurations" we encounter, along with 2 that are often confused with CoMITs:

1. **Workstation CoMITs.** Servers & Infrastructure versus Workstations & End Users. Most common CoMITs setup for us. The MSP handles the servers and infrastructure and you (the CoMITs Internal IT Folks) handle workstations and users.

2. **Server CoMITs.** Workstations & End Users versus Servers & Infrastructure. The reverse of scenario #1. The MSP handles the workstations and end-users, you handle the servers and infrastructure.

3. **Full CoMITs.** (aka "In Case of Fire…") At first, this looks like Monitoring Only, but you'd be mistaken. You are responsible for all IT issues using the MSP's STMPs.

4. **Silo.** When a 3rd party is offering specific skills and only those skills, it's tempting to consider them as a form of CoMITs. In my opinion, not so much. Don't get me wrong, we do a lot of SQL-based Silo work with customers. But those customers aren't getting the full benefits of CoMITs through the shared STMPs or the like.

5. **Monitoring Only.** This was extremely popular about 5 or so years ago. It was touted as a great way for MSPs to get their foot into the door for clients. The MSP would provide the monitoring of the network and would charge extra to take any action on anything. We've talked with several potential CoMITs clients who had a "monitoring only" agreement with an MSP. Every single one had the same observation. They'd get the alerts, and the MSP would simply say "if you want us to fix it, it'll cost you extra." Not a very good relationship building strategy, if you ask me. And certainly not CoMITs as we define it.

Let's talk briefly about why each of the first 3 choices might appeal to you:

- **Workstation CoMITs.** If you really work well with the end-users and the desktops but don't have the best handle on servers (including virtualization, backups, configurations, RAID, etc.). We've found this to be pretty common with companies that have fallen behind with their servers, companies that are still running Server 2008 10 years later and need to upgrade. Same issue with infrastructure, including switches, firewalls and the like.

- **Server CoMITs.** The opposite of Workstation CoMITs. Your internal group has a great handle on the servers and infrastructure, but don't have the bandwidth to handle end-user issues. Especially true with large organizations (in terms of end-users) where the Internal IT folks are highly skilled but low in numbers. It's also appealing for organizations with large numbers of remote users. Or they just don't like people.[41]

- **Full CoMITs.** This is where you feel that you (the Internal IT folks) can handle (armed with the STMPs) most IT issues. But it's great to have some backup when you need it.

I can't stress it enough. In each case above, both parties (you and the MSP) have access to the STMPs that are used to deal with the issue(s).

Equally important is that for the areas where you have primary responsibility, you're not alone or abandoned. Far from it.

ADVICE AND ESCALATION

As your CoMITs partner, we're in this together. We're sharing the STMPs and we've also got your back. When you run into something that you need help with, we're there with you.

The first is advice. If you run into a circumstance or situation where you're just not sure. You want to handle it yourself but want to run it by someone. Or get a thumbs up on a plan of attack. Or sanity check.

That's included. *No additional charge.* And think about it, you're asking advice from someone (um, us, the MSP) that already knows your network. Knows the same STMPs that you're using. It only needs to be brought up to speed with the specific details. We're not starting from scratch.

---

[41] As the great Tom Lehrer said, "I know that there are people who do not love their fellow man, and I hate people like that!"

The second is escalation. If you're in a situation that you want the MSP to handle the issue, just escalate the ticket. And we'll handle the issue. In this case, you will incur additional costs, usually time and materials, but it's entirely in your hands whether that is worth it or not.

The nice thing about escalation is that you can ask to be involved in the solution. If it's something that you think you'll encounter again in the future, just ask to be involved in the solution, so next time you won't have to pay to have it done for you.

Of course, you can escalate tickets for any reason. You're buried and need some temporary help clearing up your workload. There's another project you've got. You need to take a vacation.

It's all up to you.

WE'RE IN IT FOR THE MONEY

And that's ok.

We mentioned this before, there's a fixed monthly fee for the CoMITs services. You (the client) know the cost. As do we (the MSP). We're all on the same page.

You escalate tickets when you realize the benefit of us (the MSP) fixing it outweighs the cost of escalation.

Feel free to try the advice route first. See if you feel like you can take it on.

Escalating too many tickets? Talk to us about providing some training. Yes, there might be some additional cost, but it might be worth it. And since we are familiar with your situation, we can be specific to the training you might need. We might even be able to provide it.

Or consider adding full support. If you're running a Full CoMITs agreement and escalating a lot of server and infrastructure tickets, maybe switching to a Desktop CoMITs would make sense.

The bottom line is that you have options.

Interlude No. 4:
The Cyber Security Vendor

When Bob first approached my perspective on the concept of Co-Managed IT services, my wheels immediately started turning. Over the years, MSPs have been transitioning from an All You Can Eat (AYCE) business model to providing critical expertise while leveraging internal IT employees for a while but verbalizing this concept and the benefits have been nebulous...until now.

The unemployment rate for technology jobs across the United States dropped to a 20-year low of 1.3 percent in May as hiring gains were recorded in both the tech sector and across the economy, according to CompTIA's analysis of Friday's U.S. Bureau of Labor Statistics "Employment Situation"[42]. Tech unemployment is at its lowest rate since January 2000, the earliest available data from the BLS (Bureau of Labor Statistics).

With this significant talent shortage, businesses of all sizes are looking for ways to monitor and manage their internal networks and computers, while not spending exorbitant amounts of money. Furthermore, with today's increased sophistication of cybersecurity threats, the training and expertise required to thwart these attacks demand a significant (and ongoing) investment in evaluation, education, and integration. This will not get any easier.

Co-Managed IT is a win-win-win for the customer, internal IT department and the MSP that serves them. However, it requires conscious coordination between all parties involved that will help

---

[42] https://www.bls.gov/news.release/empsit.nr0.htm

achieve authentic trust where *everyone* remains comfortable, recognizes the anticipated value and achieves the expected security posture they desire so they can focus on growing their business while minimizing the risk of a company-ending breach. Therein lies the strength of the approach outlined here by Bob.

In the past, MSPs have marketed primarily at completely replacing the internal IT resources (you), or at least keeping them at arm's length in an almost adversarial or at least highly consultative relationship.

With CoMITs, the internal IT individual or team can now focus on lowering company costs in other areas and/or engage in more revenue-generating activities while improving internal operational efficiencies.

The MSP can also embrace the role of educator and security expert. While attackers are more sophisticated and difficult to detect, they also continue to find success in using some tried-and-true tactics to trick users into granting access to systems and sensitive data. This presents MSPs with the opportunity to develop and co-lead the effort to educate users on best security practices, as well as dismiss the misperception that attackers don't target small businesses. Massive data breaches against large multinational companies and national political parties make the headlines, but attackers do not discriminate.

MSPs are working more and more with internal IT teams to understand machine and deep learning and neural networks to translate that into action for SMB customers with a solution that is more predictive versus reactive.

Hackers are relentless in their quest to target organizations of all sizes with a goal to generate revenue through ransomware and acquisition of personally identifiable information, working together puts the customer in the best position for success!

Let's get equally relentless in defeating them…together!

Scott Barlow
Vice President, Global MSP
Sophos

Is CoMITs for you?

INTRODUCTION

Ok, you've taken two routes to get to this part of the book. Either you read the whole thing, or you are taking the short hike. If this section makes you think you're a fit, then you will continue to read the rest. Maybe.

Either way works for me.

My dad was an insurance salesman. By all accounts, he was a pretty good one. Every year he seemed to win awards and was quite well known in the area. He taught me two valuable lessons.

First, there was no way in hell I would ever be an insurance salesman. No, I don't need to see a counselor.

Secondly, was that he told me once that he always felt it was critical to discuss with potential clients why they shouldn't buy from him. Not everybody is a perfect fit, whether it be for a service or product or for the provider of the same. To pretend that it *is* a perfect fit for everyone is not only disingenuous but also dangerous in the long run.

CoMITs truly isn't for all MSPs. It isn't for all potential client organizations. It isn't for all Internal IT organizations. And it isn't for all Internal IT individuals.

And if it isn't? Then don't pretend it is.

For everybody's sake.

MAYBE IT IS

You want a relationship where both parties (Internal IT and the MSP) are equally engaged and committed.[43] It's either going to be a win-win or lose-lose scenario.

You are open to changing the STMPs when it makes sense for the long term of your organization.

You are open to changing your best practices with the same caveat. You want to learn.

Your organization is willing to keep IT reasonably up to date.

Your IT is primarily made up of mainstream technologies and components.

Your current IT is lacking. You need to add something, whether it be skills, capacity, components or just additional resources you can call on.

You understand the needs of the business or at least want to understand.

Your organization needs to upgrade a lot of their IT but needs to keep some legacy[44] equipment and software. Meanwhile, you know the old stuff but don't have a clue about the new.

If there are ways you could be more valuable to the company if your time was freed up from some of the more "mundane" aspects of IT, but not enough to move you completely out of operational IT.

You don't have time to keep up with the newer stuff. Oh, but the company expects you to be versed in newer technology as it pertains to the future growth of the company.

You're a one-person shop. You're already overworked, underpaid, untrained and unappreciated. And every time you bring in a seagull/ vendor to fix something, they leave you with no idea as to what they did or how to maintain it.

---

[43] Remember the pig in the ham and egg breakfast?

[44] We use the term "legacy" a lot to avoid the words "old crap". But you get the idea. Especially when the old crap still works.

If management knew how many things are hanging by a hair down here...

You're the living example of the saying "It's hard to remember to drain the swamp when you're up to your ass in alligators."

Your "to-do" list includes a lot of items that an MSP would consider low-hanging fruit. Items like end-user cybersecurity training, dark web monitoring, IT documentation, password management, multi-factor authentication. You know you should. You know you want to. You even have management understanding it's needed. All you need to accomplish these things is a month without sleep. And then for the subsequent months working with 30% less sleep. Yeah, that's the ticket!

Training would be great, but even someone to bounce ideas off would be great!

Vacations are a myth. Sick days are by the phone. Really sick days are by email. If you're in the hospital, check your text messages.

MAYBE IT ISN'T

CoMITs is first and foremost about a trusting relationship. If you don't feel that you can let your guard down with another organization, warts and all? Don't do this. If you are willing to share the fact that your documentation is lousy, then the MSP can be instrumental in helping you clean it up especially using the STMPs specifically for this issue. If you want to hold back because you don't want to look bad? That's kind of like the person who cleans their house before the cleaning folks drop by because they're embarrassed about the look of the house. Here are some other hints that CoMITs might not be for you:

- If you have information about the client, the employer, that makes you irreplaceable, does that cause you concern or do you feel it keeps you and your job secure?[45] If it's the latter, CoMITs

---

[45] Trust me, if it makes you feel more secure, that's a legitimate feeling for short term at best. And that has nothing to do with CoMITs.

isn't for you. Part of the job of the MSP is to try to minimize the risk to the client organization, and to work with you to accomplish this. Eliminating single points of failure is a big part of that. When there's a problem, do you try to find someone to blame, or work on the solution?

- You developed your own set of best practices and STMPs. They were all born out of necessity, desperation, and zero budgets. They work, but much of it works because you know "how to use them," and you or the organization is not willing to change them.

- Your company has very unusual technologies throughout the entire organization and can't change them because of business requirements. This usually doesn't work out for pure MSP solutions because MSPs work best when they can reproduce the skillsets and best practices across multiple clients, resulting in greater efficiencies and therefore lower costs. The weirder your requirements are for the MSP, the more expensive it would be to manage and maintain your environment. This works out great if the responsibilities can be split so that the Internal IT folks (that would be you) could be responsible for the unusual stuff, and the MSP handle the mainstream pieces. If you can't split them? Not so much.

- You or the management don't recognize the value of all the additional STMPs best practices and aren't open to discussion. I've had several discussions with CEO's and Internal IT folks, and actually a few MSP CEO's, oddly enough. In several cases, the topic would turn to relatively new offerings, like end-user cybersecurity training, dark web monitoring, IT documentation, password management, multi-factor authentication. Often the response was "we don't need that" or "yeah, one of these days." CoMITs brings those pieces and much more right out of the gate. If you aren't willing to entertain them, you're ignoring the values that the program brings. You are also (in some cases) keeping the organization vulnerable to a level the MSP may not be comfortable with.

- You are not willing to go to a ticketing system for your own work. We've tried CoMITs with the client not using the ticketing system. And it still...works. Just not as well. Not nearly as well.

NEXT STEPS

Introduction

So, you've read the book. At least as much as you're going to. And you're still interested?[46]

That's fantastic, but we're by no means done. The assessment and proposal process we (the MSP) go through is like what we go through with a traditional MSP opportunity. But we need to do a couple of additional things, specifically looking at the relationship that we're looking build with...well, you.

IT's not Personal

When we review your IT, we're doing it from two perspectives. First is the operational. The traditional process of making sure the lights are blinking in the right way and at the right time. The health of the devices, backups, security...all that good stuff.

The second is where it gets personal. How's the internal documentation? Ticketing process? Best practices? Skill sets of the Internal IT folks (again, that's you?)[47] Identification and prioritization of single points of failure? Relationship between IT and management?

Here's the thing. There are going to be some issues that are brought up where...well, you won't look perfect. And that's understandable.

---

[46] Well, that wasn't expected<g>

[47] Seriously, by now you would think I wouldn't have to repeat this<g>!

First, if everything was perfect, why bring us on board? Second, there are often valid reasons.[48] During this process, we will prepare you as to what things we discover and how we will discuss them with management.

Will we hide your shortcomings? Uh…no. That doesn't do anyone any good, but we'll add context to it and present these items as opportunities and develop strategies to eliminate these together.

Here's the catch. If you're truly a bad employee[49] with no interest in "reforming," then this isn't for you. The goal behind CoMITs is everybody working together.

Here are the steps. By the way, there may be several contacts or conversations between each step. Consider these milestones in the process.

Network Assessment

This is the same as with a traditional MSP opportunity. We use various tools to get a good snapshot of the current IT environment. Usually, this generates a ton of reports.

IT Assessment

This is specific to the CoMITs process. Think of it as a review of the health of you (Internal IT folks) and your approach to your job, but not in a criticizing way.

Informal Findings/Proposal Review

Boy, this is critical. We review the findings and the preliminary proposal with you, and only you. This is where we show you all the findings (good and bad). We discuss why things are the way they are

---

[48] The one most common is lack of priority from management, aka "It's hard to drain the swamp when you're up to your ass in alligators".

[49] In the 12 years we've been in business, I can only really think of 2 circumstances where we've dealt with this situation.

and some strategies about cleaning them up. In some cases, we even talk about why they might be that way on purpose. More than once we've found legacy software that's incredibly out of date, only to find that it *must* be that way because of legacy equipment. The equipment is running fine but would cost a small fortune to upgrade. This is a great example of how your internal knowledge combined with ours moves mountains.

We also present to you our preliminary proposal (and strategy behind it).

The goal is for us to be in synch with our proposal and approach. In all honesty, if we can't come to an agreement, we probably won't move forward to present to management.

Formal Proposal Review

Now, we present to the decision-makers. Together. If we've[50] done our due diligence, neither of us should be surprised by anything the other will say.

ONBOARDING

Onboarding usually takes from 30-45 days, which will include training for you and your folks on the STMPs that you'll be learning. There's also communication with the rest of your organization. This should come from you. You're not going anywhere. You're still the face/voice of IT.

We create an onboarding project and work together to implement it. Our starting point is a templated project plan that includes:[51]

1. **Gather Initial Information**
   a. **Review Risk/Expectations.** This process reviews expectations, risks, assumptions for both sides during onboarding.

---

[50] By "we," I mean you and the MSP.
[51] These tasks are not necessarily performed sequentially

    b. **Transitional information.** Gathering of information such as ISP info, licensing, domain registrar

    c. **Business Operational.** Specific business requirements. Off-hour needs. Who can submit tickets? Who can request changing of a user password?

    d. **Specific STMPs details.** Some STMPs have implementation options, determine preliminary requirements.

2. **Verify current backup health.** The last line of defense in all bad things IT is a good backup.

3. **Communicate to Organization.** There will be a change. Some of it will be welcome,[52] some of it will be painful.[53] Communicate with the premise of "Under promise and Over deliver."

4. **Implement STMPs.** This can also involve removing former STMPs.

5. **STMP Training.** Yes, there is training. Some of it is online and can be taken at your leisure.

As you might expect, there's a lot more detail to onboarding, but you get the idea.

---

[52] Take the credit!

[53] Blame us (the MSP)!

Interlude No. 5: The IT Technician

When our IT Manager informed us that he was retiring, we started the process of finding a new IT Manager. 7 months later, we had gone through 3 people. We decided to change direction at that point and focused on an IT outside firm (MSP). We interviewed a couple of firms. Simplex-IT stood out to us. Bob explained to us how they operate. It seemed like a good fit. We were right.

Bob explained that they were not there to take over all the IT duties. He explained the idea of CoMITS. It sounded like a great concept. One of the first things they put in place was to backup all our servers to the cloud. This was a first for us, but we put our trust in Simplex-IT.

Don't get me wrong, we have had a couple of hiccups but nothing we couldn't work together and fix. Simplex-IT has become an extension of our company. You must Trust and Communicate or this will not work.

We can concentrate on moving forward while Simplex-IT takes care of challenges that come up. If we have an issue, we can set up a call to answer our questions and or concerns. Simplex-IT also educates. Education is power. And they give you a lot of power. To this point in our adventure with Simplex-IT has been a great ride.

Thanks to Bob, Kevin, Kurt, Adam, Jessica, Joel and all the others at Simplex-IT.

Jerry Traugh
IT Technician
Everhard Products Inc.

Conclusion

Well, here we are. The end of the book. I hope this hasn't been a complete waste of time. More importantly, I hope I was able to lead you through the mental exercise of determining whether CoMITs would benefit you as an IT professional, as well as, your organization. Honestly, I don't care if your conclusion was "yes" or "no". My concern is that you have good reasons for your conclusion. If you do, then this book has hopefully helped you to that conclusion.

Feel free to reach to me with questions, comments or concerns at Bob@Simplex-IT.com.